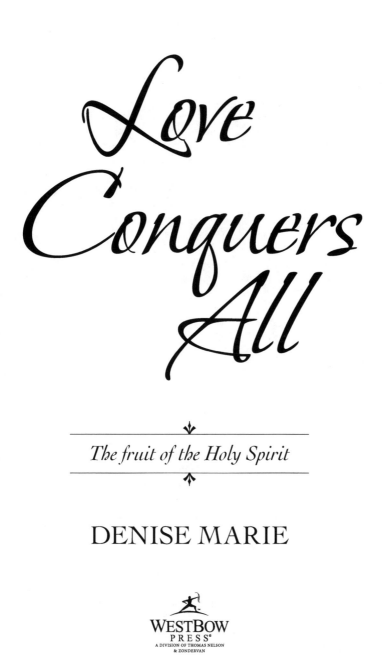

Love Conquers All

The fruit of the Holy Spirit

DENISE MARIE

WESTBOW
P R E S S®
A DIVISION OF THOMAS NELSON
& ZONDERVAN

WestBow Press books may be ordered through
booksellers or by contacting:

WestBow Press
A Division of Thomas Nelson & Zondervan
1663 Liberty Drive
Bloomington, IN 47403
www.westbowpress.com
844-714-3454

ISBN: 978-1-6642-2603-6 (sc)
ISBN: 978-1-6642-2602-9 (e)

Print information available on the last page.

WestBow Press rev. date: 03/03/2021

This book is dedicated to all of God's children, especially those that love God with a sincere heart. I'm also writing this book to let all that read it know how important it is for us to know and recognize the love of God, the voice of God, and the word of God. It is also important to recognize the need to have a relationship with Jesus Christ. I began writing this book after a long hard war I went through in my body called Lupus. At the time I was 57 years young, and could not understand why I was so fatigued and worn out all of the time.

LOVE CONQUERS ALL

*T*his near constant state of fatigue began suddenly one day, (I believe it was around August 6, 2013)as I was getting ready to go to work. As I was getting ready for work, I became dizzy, but not giving it a thought, I kept on getting dressed and went to work. About two hours into that work day, I experienced another bout of dizziness, and a more than usual amount of fatigue. From that point on, I struggled to overcome this overwhelming wave of fatigue, as I fought to finish working my shift.

The next day I made an appointment with the doctor, and was scheduled to see him later that week. The doctor told me my red blood count was too low and he gave me a blood transfusion and let me go home. Within two weeks, I felt the same dizziness and fatigue as I did before the blood transfusion. I called my doctor and explained my symptoms, and he told me to go to the emergency room. After the initial symptoms assessment, the emergency room doctor admitted me into the hospital to run tests. I was so distraught while in the hospital bed, that I couldn't help but wonder if the Lord was ready to call me home. I laid there praying, asking the Lord to clean me up spiritually and emotionally so that I would be ready to meet Him in peace. I knew that I needed to pray further, but I was so frightened and confused that I wasn't quite sure what to say. After settling down for a moment and clearing my mind, I asked the Lord for his guidance. I felt my inner self begin to speak to me and tell me what I needed to say when I prayed. As the words of prayer formed in my mind, I knew it was the Lord that was putting them there. I began to silently pray, "dear Lord, help the doctors treat my body, so I can be a living testament to your glory and your will." There is a verse in the Bible, (See Philippians 4:6) that tells us not to be anxious for nothing, but pray and make your requests known to God. Although some Christians maintain that they have never heard the voice of God, I'm here to tell everybody the voice of God is real! I did say those words in my prayer exactly as the Lord said them to me. Some time later, I presumed that all of the test results were in, because I could see my doctor standing outside of my room talking to some other doctors while they were all looking at pieces of paper, which I surmised were my test results. After about 15 minutes of what I presume was a team discussion about my test results, the doctors gathered just outside of my room armed with the test results in their hands. I felt a sense of foreboding and dread, as the team of doctors,(each probably some kind of specialist in their respective fields) came into my room, and gathered around my hospital room bed. So many thoughts whirled through my mind. Did I have cancer?

Heart disease? Was I going home that day? What would the diagnosis be? Before my imagination carried me further down into a valley of uncertainty and fear, my primary care doctor entered the room. As my doctor entered the room, I sought to read the rigid expression on his face for a clue...any clue, was it going to be good news, bad news? Seeing nothing in his eyes or in the expression on his face, I realized I was going to have to wait until he told me the diagnosis. Finally the moment of truth was upon me, all was about to be revealed. As my doctor opened his mouth to speak, I braced myself for the impact of what he would say to me. It suddenly became very quiet in my room, as I became intently focused on what he was going to say. Finally, he delivered the diagnosis by saying: "you have systemic lupus in your blood system". The blank look on my face must have signaled to him that he needed to tell me in plain non-medical English what "systemic lupus" meant. Straining to find the right words, my doctor haltingly explained that "systemic lupus" meant my red blood cells were fighting against my white blood cells, which was rapidly turning my good blood into bad blood and stopping my kidneys from functioning correctly.

The clinical implications and prognosis of "systemic lupus" eluded me, but one thing I did understand with crystal clarity is that, there was a war going on in my body literally between my red blood cells, and white blood cells. After adjusting somewhat to the initial shock of the diagnosis, I noticed for the first time, the anguished and saddened look on my doctor's face. I began to feel that the "cat was out of the bag:" a death sentence had been uttered without being said. The expression on my doctor's face changed as he took off his professional "face mask" and looked me in the eyes. At that moment, I saw a fellow human, not a doctor, looking me in the eyes. The unspoken death sentence quietly stood in the corner of the room not wanting its presence to be acknowledged. After what seemed like an eternity, I finally summoned the courage to acknowledge this unseen stranger in the corner. I had been praying with all confidence, and I was certain that our Lord was not going to abandon me now, so I looked my doctor in the eyes and asked; "Are there any procedures to fix the problem?" Maybe it was the sincerity in my voice or a perceived child like innocence in the straight forward manner in which I asked the question, but the effect changed his entire mood. As the sad mask fell from my doctor's face, I sensed that there was a glimmer of hope, a small light shining at the end of a dark medical tunnel, but a light nevertheless! With a seemingly renewed sense of purpose and enthusiasm, my doctor started to perk up, and went on to tell me about the new procedures and treatments that were available for systemic lupus. After a lengthy discussion about the procedures they would use, my doctor ended the discussion by emphasizing that medical science could not, at this time promise a favorable outcome. Resigned to my fate, and realizing that the outcome of any treatment was now firmly in the Lord's hands, I said: "Ok," as we shook hands and he left the room. I began to talk to the Lord and thank Him for guiding me and giving me the words to say in prayer, when I needed his assurance and guidance the most. I didn't realize at the time that it wasn't a long prayer, but it was the right prayer at the right time. Although that prayer was just a few words, I could sense God's presence right there with me, when I needed Him the most. It was the love of God that came down to protect me even before the beginning of my time. As a result of my Biblical readings and research, I have come to the conclusion that one word and concept seems to repeat itself throughout the Bible in many different ways. That word and concept is "love." Love, however, is not just a word that the human race should take lightly because It's a word with action through the Holy Spirit.

Since I started writing this book the demon known as Corona virus 19 has reared its ugly head. In January of 2020, the corona virus had not yet risen to the level of public awareness. Accordingly, when I went to the hospital about January 8, with flu like symptoms, the doctors said I had a very bad case of the flu. I suspect that since the medical staff was aware of my history of lupus, they decided to admit me as an inpatient. After enduring an arduous treatment regimen which spanned about 7 days, I was discharged and sent home. About 3 days later, I began to have trouble breathing so I called my doctor. An appointment was made for me to come to his office the next day. I have an ongoing lung condition called Chronic Obstructive Pulmonary Disease(COPD) and although I was prescribed medication to treat it, I hadn't felt the need to use the medication for about 2 years. I told my doctor about not taking the formerly prescribed medication, and he gave me a different medicine for the COPD. After taking the new medication for a few days, I noticed a marked improvement with my breathing such that I was able to resume my normal activities. In March of 2020 the corona virus was formally announced to the American public, and the symptoms and means of transmission explained. Ironically, I noticed that the symptoms that were described, were the same symptoms I had, that the medical staff had labeled as influenza. I must emphasize again that I never stopped praying for God's help, from the time I got sick all the way until the time I went to the doctor because I never did feel well until I started taking the newly prescribed COPD medicine.

I look at life this way: if you do right, when you ask Jesus to come to your rescue he will be there to help you, regardless of how difficult we perceive our situation to be. We are born of flesh, and as such, are susceptible to the weariness and despair the great trials and tribulations life takes us through. Life is a process, but with the help of God, somehow we are able to persevere. I thank God that he allowed me to get the corona virus, and healed me before the hospitals and medical staff were over run with coronavirus patients as they are now. (March 30th 2020.)

$\mathbf{\Psi}$

THE FRUIT OF THE SPIRIT

$\mathbf{\uparrow}$
---

*T*here are nine fruit of the Holy Spirit. In Galatians chapter 5 the first verse tells us to stand fast in the liberty that Christ has made us free, and be not entangled again in bondage. The 22nd verse of Galatians names the fruit of the Spirit as "Love, joy, Peace, Long suffering, Gentleness, Goodness, Faith, Meekness and Temperance against such there is no law." I believe in his infinite wisdom, God has given all humans a measure of these characteristics. It is up to each individual to implement the fruit of the Holy Spirit in their everyday lives. The fruit of the spirit are the characteristics Christians exhibit once they allow the Holy Spirit to work in their lives. In order to experience the fruit of the Holy Spirit, Christians must surrender themselves to the guidance of the Holy Spirit, as we can not do it alone. When the Holy Spirit completely controls the life of a believer, he produces the fruit of the Holy Spirit.

The manner in which we regard the first three fruit of the spirit(love, joy, and peace) are commensurate with our attitude towards God. The first fruit, love, is something the Christian experiences as a sort of growth process. That is to say, love of God, love of our brothers and sisters, and love of God's creations grows as we grow to better understand God's plan.

Although joy and happiness are two separate words, most believe they are synonymous. joy comes from the Holy Spirit. joy is something that Christians achieve only after devoting themselves to a complete belief in the Holy Spirit. Happiness on the other hand, is a feeling that waxes and wanes for most people, because it is a form of self contentment that may be generated with or without the Holy Spirit. Happiness may be viewed as a state of contentment with one's self and one's surroundings. Happiness in one form or another, is something we wait for, look for and hope to have one day.

Peace is not only an absence of war, it is a freedom from quarrels and disagreements with other men. God's peace binds us to live in a state of peace with all men. The next three fruit of the Spirit, Long-Suffering, Gentleness and Goodness, have to do with social relationships. Long-Suffering is the ability to bear and endure hardship. In times of personal crises, the Christian calls upon the Holy Spirit to help him bear and endure the many stresses brought about by interpersonal interactions with family, coworkers, or other people in our everyday lives.

Gentleness is a quality of tenderness. Goodness is a quality of moral expectancy and wisdom. We cannot truly honestly act on these qualifications continually without the Holy Spirit. "There is none good but God." (Mark 10:18).

The last three principles that guide a Christian's conduct are Faith, Meekness and Temperance. We have to have Faith to believe that Jesus Christ died on the cross for our sins. Having Faith in the Lord is a major part of a Christian's life.

Meekness is required of those who would be called "the elect of God." (Colossians 3:12) Meekness is to have a humbled mind towards one another.

Temperance allows the Christian to resist being ruled by worldly displays of behavior and expression. Temperance is also manifested by the ability to meter one's desires before indulging in worldly acts. Temperance requires that the Christian do everything in moderation in the shadow of the Holy Spirit. The application of temperance in our daily lives also serves to further remind the Christian what is expected of him and how he is to conduct himself in the sea of worldly temptations and desires. The Christian should also bear in mind that adherence to the principles of Faith, Meekness and Temperance requires great self discipline and spiritual strength that we can find with the help of the Lord.

🌿 Love

Nearly every person on earth can lay claim to being in love or having loved another person at some time in their lives. However, do we really know what love is? Do we have any idea about the origin of love? It may come as a shock to some to learn that love comes from God. "God is love."(1 John 4:8) Jesus said: "If you love me, keep my commands."(John 14:15) Regarding love, we ask, what is Jesus' commandment? Jesus' commandment regarding love is "That ye love one another; as I have loved you, that ye also love one another."(John 13:34)

"Love" has been broadly classified by man as falling into three categories: Philos Love, Agape Love, and Eros Love. Philos Love is the love we have for one another, e.g., the love between a husband and wife. Brotherly love may be thought of as the love siblings have for each other. Agape Love is the divine love that God, our creator, has for all men and women. When Jesus came to save mankind from sin, He had to humble Himself in love. Jesus is the son of God, and as such, is the best example of love man will ever have.

"Eros" is derived from ancient Greek, meaning love or desire. Eros Love can therefore be translated into the English words: desire and longing.("Eros" was also the name of the god of love in ancient Greece.) "Eros love" can also be viewed as an erotic love that is selfish and associated with sexual love. Eros love is mostly based on self-benefits. Eros love always seeks to "control and conquer" and this drive is most acutely felt at the beginning of a relationship. Eros love is also based on the physical man and woman that God created to come together in marriage as one. God did not intend love to be selfish.

🌿 More about Agape Love

So let's talk about Agape love now that we know God is love. One aspect of agape love, is the love God has for his creation, mankind.("For God so loved the world..." John 3:16) Another aspect of agape love, is the love we show to one another. We can garner more information about agape love by reading the Bible. (See 2 Peter 1:7, Romans 5:8, etc.) In order to fully understand, and live by the principle of Agape love, we must first of all, humble ourselves towards one another. We must further renounce strife, by avoiding unnecessary altercation, and reasoning with one another regardless of who is right or who is wrong. The concept of compromise should be used to come to an agreement, that the other party should accept. In lieu of compromise, we may come to an amicable agreement to "agree to disagree." This is the kind of love Christians should seek to achieve on a daily basis. A Christian should seek peace with all men and Holiness, because when one says "I am a Christian" one should show it in their everyday life. A faithful Christian has to remember that he is being held to a higher standard of conduct in the eyes of the world, and carry himself accordingly. Any faltering or lapse of conduct that is less than Christ like, will be viewed as not only human frailty on your part, but as a denunciation of Christ, the Bible and Christians in general.

We were created to love no matter what, human nature is one of love without dissimulation. We are all accountable for our own actions. And therein lies the difference between following God and making your own decisions. Love should be free in your heart. Love that flows unending is unconditional love, it is measureless. This is the kind of love Jesus showed when he came down from his throne, in the likeness of man, to show mankind the way to get back with God. In some situations, it is sometimes, (out of love for our fellow man) better to not speak a word and let things work themselves out, than to continue to prolong conflict. Non contention based on love should be uppermost in your mind, especially if you are a believer in Christ. We should trust and believe that God will carry us though every situation. We must remember that Jesus did not die on the cross for selfish reasons, he died out of love for mankind. Jesus came to us with a clean and pure heart, and that's the way we should go to Him when we leave this world. The world did not like Jesus and the world is not going to like those of us that believe in Him.

The scriptures tell us that "God is love." (See 1 John 4:8) If we believe that God is love, we should endeavor to have a close relationship with God, that we may love more fully. To have a relationship with God is to know who Jesus is. To establish a relationship with God we should; be a doer of the word of God, use every opportunity to go out and share what we have learned about God's word with people we come in contact with, and finally we should always pray, not only when we need something, but as a way of keeping our connection with God and getting closer to Jesus as well. Reading God's word in the Bible on a daily basis, as much as possible, is another way to cement our relationship with God. God has given us all "assignments" in life, i.e., things he expects us to do, and we have a duty to complete our "assignments," if we are indeed true followers of his word. Adherence to the aforementioned principles will start the believer on the road to getting to know what assignment he has been given as an individual believer. Everyone has his/her own work to do in the Lord. The Lord has given us all different talents to complete our "assignments", and accordingly, some are to destined to be teachers, others will become preachers, still others will become apostles, prophets, interpreters of tongues, evangelists, and so on.

🕸 What about Love

Love is expressed in a variety of ways including thoughts, fantasies, and beliefs which serve to value behavioral roles and relationships. These thoughts, fantasies and beliefs may manifest themselves in biological, physical, social, emotional and spiritual ways. The biological and physical aspect of sexuality largely concerns human reproduction, which includes the human sexual response cycle and is a basic biological drive that exists in all species. Physical and emotional aspects of sexuality that form a bond between individuals are expressed through profound feelings and physical manifestations of love, trust and care. The Social aspects of love deal with the way humans interact with each other in society. Spiritual aspects of love may be seen in individuals who are spiritually connected with others. Sexuality also impacts, and is impacted by cultural, political, philosophical, moral, ethnic and religious aspects of life. Sexual activity is a vital principle of human living and as such is responsible for activating the pleasure centers of the brain, which in turn control the energy of the body. The knowledge of human intimacy is known to most of us as a form of love. Opinions differ as to the nature of individual sexual behavior. Some think sexuality is determined by genetics, while others believe sexual behavior is modeled by the individual's environment. Others believe both of these could impact the behavioral form of a child.

What on earth does love have to do with sex? Here again, we must ask ourselves do we know the origin of love, or even what love is? Sometimes in the Bible people had sex for the express purpose of procreation. Procreation however, was not always the goal of having sex. When Abraham lay with Hagar, she conceived Ishmael, when Jacob laid with Leah, she conceived Ruben. However, were these people in love when they had sex? Technically having sex does not mean making love because we don't have to love someone to have sex with them. We cannot "make" love. Love comes from God.

The thing about love is before we reach puberty, (for some of us) family love is all we know. By the time puberty is just about over, and we begin to spread our wings of independence, we are not around our family members as much. We find that it's time to open another door as we begin to spread our wings of love to encompass others. This love of others was already within us, it's just another identity of love of which we are unaware until the time arrives to unleash it. We could very well say coming out of puberty is an entryway into adulthood. Of course there are more steps before a person actually reaches the peak of adulthood. Just because a person is sexually mature, doesn't necessarily mean they're sexually active. Also just because a young person is sexually active doesn't mean that person is an adult. At this stage of young adulthood, as we symbolically close one door and open another, we learn love extends farther than our immediate family. We also learn that because we love someone in a certain way, doesn't mean that love will be returned in the same way. After a while we learn that holding on to unreturned love while hoping for a change sometimes has advantages and disadvantages. Throughout history humans have been trying to determine what is love, establish how we should love, identify the reason for love, and observe love along with many other reasons. However, know for sure that God is love!!!

LOVE AND COMMITMENT

When we talk about commitment there are responsibilities that follow. Commitment is largely the love in a relationship between two or more people. When one repents of one's sins, that's a commitment to Jesus. However, we must keep in mind that there are a variety of commitments. It is said Eros love is selfishness and mostly associated with non commitment and sexual lusts. It is also said this kind of love is mostly based on self benefit, and usually control is what one or both partners are seeking. Sometimes there is no shame in letting the partner know that he or she wants to be in control of the relationship. No matter what is said or done the controlling partner wants to have the final say in the relationship. This is known to us as Erotic love and is understood to be based on intuition or "love at first sight." This type of love has to do with chemistry matching the sexual tendencies of each other at the same time. It is said most of the time that when erotic love turns into marriage, it's hard work. Once the erotic flames of sex die down, the marriage usually dies with it, because the marriage was based on sex and lust.

When we think of love we think of deep affection, fondness, of a romantic and sexual attachment to another person that another person cares for. Love can also be thought of as adoration, idolization, and blind devotion. In the human mind there are many different ways to love. Once we believe love comes from the being of the Creation, it could only mean love comes from within(i.e., the Soul).

Consider that we take it for granted that our hearts pump blood throughout our bodies, and we know that our bodies cannot live without blood. Love then, may be considered the "spiritual blood" of the soul, and like our bodies without blood, spiritually the soul will surely die without love. Our souls are condemned to wander in eternal darkness without love. While in that state of darkness, some people protect their loved ones, some cover-up love for many different reasons, some commit to love, and some are afraid to commit to love. Trusting is as vital to love as red blood cells are to white blood blood cells. We say love comes from the heart because in order for us to exist in the body we have to have blood pumping in and out of our heart. Others however, say love comes from the brain. According to science, there is a chemical reaction in the brain that has something to do with our chemistry toward one another. This chemical reaction makes us think we have a special love for another person, or when we see someone, that takes our breath away at first sight, we feel love. As we learned in school, the functions of all our actions and reactions that govern our physical bodies occur in the brain. With that being said, I'll say love is a chemical reaction in the brain that occurs when we think we are in love. This type of chemical reaction generates the love of attraction, lust and attachment. When we experience this kind of reaction, we say that we love someone.

Many people may define Non-Commitment of love as simply love without commitment. Other people may profess that being in love is a temporary state that is usually NOT everlasting. In contrast to this however, there are others that may think being in love IS everlasting. The idea of being committed in a love relationship could make someone fearful of love for many reasons. A person may have had parents or known people that did not show love, in what was supposed to be a love relationship. Following the flawed model that they have based their ideas of love upon, these people are afraid to show love. We think we are capable of handling love ourselves, but we don't want to go through the emotions of love's ups and downs. We have all seen examples of love that was shown to be not true and faithful. Some people have experienced a lot of hurt from loved ones, and some people think it just takes too much strength and effort to commit to love. Committing to love is not something of the past, love was here before man ever was and it will be here eternally.

There are gestures and ways that a person uses to signal good intentions and feelings towards loved ones. That doesn't mean there's a commitment from the person giving or receiving the gesture even though one or the other may think so. Anxiety, probably has a lot to do with someone who is chronically unable to make a commitment. A sense of impending loss, based on the fear of a committed relationship is also another reason people tend to avoid engaging in committed love relationships. Not being able to express this fear results in a breakdown of communication between the two parties, resulting in a non committed love relationship. At that point in the relationship, either one or both of the parties may experience an attack of anxiety. It is written in 2nd Timothy 1:7-8: "For God has not given us the spirit of fear but of power and love and of a sound mind." What that means in this context, is that what we fail to realize is that there are many options available to us, because there are so many potential avenues from which we can choose. Commitment is a part of life, almost everything we do involves or becomes some type of commitment. Going to work, going to school, going to church, etc., are all routine life commitments. Behind almost everything we do lurks the danger involved with the fear of non-commitment. Some of the more common of these fears may encompass loneliness, (which breeds an unhealthy state of mind), emotional trauma, and hopelessness.

Let's delve into the concept of non commitment a little deeper by using as an example of a woman named LaQuisha. When she met the future father of her children she thought she found the love of her life. She thought their relationship would last forever. Over the course of several years, they had several children together, and through hard work and perseverance had arrived at a comfortable station in life. The relationship seemed solid and everything else appeared to be going well, until he asked her to marry Him. She refused, saying,"Why do we need to get married?!, We have a family, and life has been good to us without marriage, there is no need for marriage!" She was happy with the non committed relationship she had, even after the births of several children. In examining LaQuisha's past, we find that she had been married once before but had not had any children. During the course of her marriage, circumstances changed, feelings withered, until her marriage was just a ghost of its former self. LaQuisha resolved that she could not continue to live in misery, so she got a divorce. After suffering the pain and heartbreak of divorce she promised herself she would not marry again. She loves her children's father very much, but she was afraid of what she saw as the probable negative consequences that the commitment of marriage would bring about. Ecclesiastes 9:9 says, "Marriage is a lifelong commitment." However the thoughts of marriage, in her mind didn't fit in with commitment.

We overcome fearfulness of commitment after one admits there is a problem of commitment. Our mind and thoughts are the only parts of our being over which we have some (not all) control, meaning we may exercise free will. If you are a Spirit filled Christian, and find yourself filled with a fear of commitment, it's time to take a step back, and think; "Why do I feel this way?" If fear is influencing your thoughts to a marked degree, there should be a desire to conquer that fear that is tormenting you. We can to some extent control our fears, and in the role of our own self tormentor, we can take control and vanquish those fears. Be aware that the solutions to, and mastery of the fears that reside within us all, are within us. Quoting President Franklin D. Roosevelt, "We have nothing to fear but fear itself," was as approbo in 1933, as it is today. Fear can be conquered by the love of God through Jesus Christ. We all have the love of God within us. "I can do all things through Christ who strengthens me." (Philippians 4:13). Now think of the spiritual aspect of fear. Once you've made up your mind to commit to something, whether it be a cause or a person, nothing can stop you from stepping out against that which you fear. Fear comes in many forms. For some, the fear of meeting people is insurmountable, for others the fear of being in a crowd is overwhelming, others may have a fear of not being able to say "no," to a certain person. One strategy of mastering our fears is to walk out on faith with respect. For example, if one is afraid of walking into a crowded room, walk into that crowded room, relax and don't focus on yourself. Harness your fear by focusing on the other people around you, by engaging in conversation or actively listening to a discussion. It is also good to talk to someone about your fears as well. Discussing your fears brings about an understanding about their nature, and in this way, one builds up the confidence to overcome these fears.

Fear and love cannot live in the same house. "House" in this context refers to being within a person. When we read God's words, it tells us about conquering fear with love. Proverbs 4:23 tells us that our life is shaped by our thoughts. No matter how we look at the situation of fear and commitment from an outside vantage point, we must ultimately examine the state and basis of these fears by looking into our own minds. Fear is a thought or feeling that keeps our minds in a tormented state. In James 1:8, it is written that "a double minded man is unstable in all his ways." This may be explained by keeping in mind that, as Christians we have to keep our mind in a controllable state through our Lord and Savior Jesus Christ. It's not so much that we're keeping our mind by ourselves, but we are asking the Lord to keep our minds. When we fear to commit, fear itself keeps us from committing and that's not the mind that the Lord Jesus wants for His people.

OFTEN PRAY

I often wish I mean I pray
If there is a will there's a way
Is there really any need to say
The way was paved the way was made
I often wish I mean I pray
My light would outshine my shade
I believe it will it will someday
I often wish I mean I pray
—Durand Huggins

❧ Joy

Joy is attained only by the Holy Spirit that dwells within. When we look up the word "joy" in the dictionary, it doesn't give us the biblical definition. The dictionary tells us joy is happiness and it is an English word. joy and happiness however, are not necessarily the same thing. The dictionary tells us happiness is based on how well things are going in the moment. joy is gladness, an emotion by the Holy Spirit, exceptionally wonderful, it comes from being filled with the Holy Spirit. Our first joy comes when we repent of our sins and ask God to create within us a clean and open heart. (Psalm 51:8,12) King David asked God for mercy and forgiveness when he acknowledged the weight of his sins.(Psalm 51:1-2, Psalm 51:3-5) David further cries out to God "restore to me the joy of your salvation"(Psalm 51:12a) When a person begins to seek the Lord and meditate on the ways of Christ, after repenting of their sins, a relationship takes place with that person and Christ. That's when the joy of the Lord comes alive by the fruit of the Holy Spirit.

Once a person begins to live a life as a Christian, the liberty of joy sometimes seems as though it begins to dissipate. This does not mean joy has left that person. Once a person receives the Holy Spirit, it never leaves; it's always there waiting for you, in the role of a Christian, to step back in place. Trying to get closer to God, may lead to some disappointment and frustration. This only means that the devil sees that you are trying to be a true Christian and is trying to disrupt your Christian faith. When you sense the devil is about to put his hand on your shoulder, brush it off, and get back to your Christian lifestyle. Just remember the very thought of the things that you used to do could take your mind away from the things of Christ. That's called losing sight of your walk with Christ. When we take our mind off of Christ, we begin to lose true life. In John 10:10, Jesus said Thieves come to "steal, kill and to destroy;" but he came that we "might have life and have it more abundantly." Time itself sometimes takes the mind to a place that it should not be, but if we keep our minds in the place that Jesus wants, it will be such that we can always reach back for the joy that dwells within. On the road to Jesus, there will be stumbling blocks, some of which will be clearly seen and some of which will be hidden. That's why it is important for us to read, study our Bible and pray everyday. Basking daily in the light of the Lord by reading the scriptures is what sustains us. Scriptural study also gives a Christian the knowledge he needs to take charge of whatever situation comes up before Him. A Believer cannot ever allow himself to get tired of praying, meditating, and reading the Bible. A believer must never cease asking the Lord what to do, which way to go, or how to do something. Trust in the Lord and the realization of his wise counsel, and we will realize where our joy comes from. We should also not forget to follow his instructions, because after we ask God's counsel, we don't always follow His instructions.

One may ask a question: "How do I know I have joy dwelling inside of me?" Once a person repents of their sins and believes in their heart without a doubt that Jesus is Lord over all, that person receives the Holy Spirit. Once you receive the Holy Spirit, that wakes up the fruit of the Spirit of God within you. I believe before we receive the Holy Spirit we already have the Fruit of the Spirit dwelling in our lives. Without the Holy Spirit we cannot use the Fruit of the Spirit to fullness. The Fruit of the Spirit gives us strength in joy and the courage to enjoy, the life that overflows, into everlasting joy. In Jesus we live and move and have our being. The testimony of a blasphemous man can not doubt the existence of God's creation. When we repent, consent to baptism(and really mean it), "in the name of Jesus Christ, for the forgiveness of our sins," we will "receive the gift of the Holy Spirit." (Acts 2:38)

To a nonbeliever true joy is incomprehensible because joy is Supernatural, and the carnal mind is empty towards God. The Holy Spirit would not leave a person once that person has repented and accepted the Lord and believes in Jesus. When Jesus comes in, joy comes in, and in the form of a work in progress, it is the Christian that changes, not God. God's love and mercy was, is and will forevermore be the same. "According to the grace of God, which is given unto me, as a wise masterbuilder, I have laid the foundation, and another buildeth thereon. But let every man take heed how he buildeth thereupon. For other foundation can no man lay than that is laid, which is Jesus Christ." (Corinthians 3:10,11) Jesus Christ teaches each how to build their foundation through Him. Once the Holy Spirit enters into a person's life, strength and courage begin to build up the hope of joy in your life. When the Holy Spirit enters your life, stress, worry, and all the other opposites of joy begin to flee from your life. The Bible tells us to "submit yourselves therefore to God. Resist the devil, and he will flee from you." (James 4:7) When you submit yourself to God, strength and courage begin to increase ten fold.

It never hurts to smile at someone when you walk past them. Because the joy that's in you could be the reason that makes their day. You are letting "your light shine before men, that they may see your good works, and glorify the Father which is in heaven." (Matthew 5:16). The source of your light is all in the power of prayer and waiting for Jesus to come to your rescue. Jesus will be there on his time, not ours. As Christians we should think on the joy that Jesus had to have to accomplish the goal that was set before Him, that is, going to Calvary to die on a cross for our sins. Crucifixion certainly wasn't a pleasant thing to endure, but shortly before his physical body expired, he said, "it is finished."(John 19:30) Glory be to God!!! Jesus was transformed from this world and sent back to the Father where he came from in the beginning of time. That's why in Romans 12:2, Paul tells us to be "transformed by the renewing of your mind."

Joy is not given by earthly material, costly array, nor pleasures of men. The greatest reason to be joyful is to please God and to spend eternity with Him. God wants us to be joyful not some of the time, but all of the time, even though he knows it's not possible in this world, but it's also not impossible if we try. The joy of the Lord is our strength. We have to allow the Holy Spirit to light up the joy in our lives.

❧ Peace

Peace is a spiritual state of tranquility and quietness. Peace, in its fullest sense can only be obtained by the Fruit of the Holy Spirit. The world does not have peace therefore the world cannot give the power of peace. We can see this disruption of peace by considering the awful effects of the Corona 19 virus. How often are we told that everything would be back the way it was before the virus? In spite of media promises of a return to the norm, death rates go up by the day. "For when they shall say, Peace and Safety;

then sudden destruction comes upon them, as travail upon a woman with child; and they shall not escape." (1 Thessalonians 5:3) We cannot obtain total peace on our own. Peace comes after we acknowledge Jesus for who he is and what he has done for our sins. When a person opens his/her heart to accept and believe Jesus died on the cross for the salvation of mankind, the peace of God is now active in his/her life. Achieving the peace of God however, is a personal and individual experience. There are many diversities of spirits in the world today. There is, however, only one Spirit of truth, and that truth is the Spirit of God. How fortunate we are that the peace within is the peace God intended for mankind.

Once a person becomes a Christian, one learns peace is a part of salvation. You don't have to wait until trials come into your life to seek the peace of God. To activate the peace within you, all you have to do is ask God for it. Through Jesus you have to take charge of your life. Taking charge of your life will keep your concentration on the goals Jesus has set for you. Traveling on the road to acknowledging the Lord as your personal Savior might require that you forgo a meal or two by fasting. Now it's time to miss a meal or two knowingly by giving that time to the Lord by fasting, praying, and reading your Bible. Your life will truly change when you allow Jesus to take charge. It's called meditating and growing in the knowledge of the Lord Jesus Christ. Meditating also allows you to get closer to God as well. Praying is also important to the service of Christ. A Christian ought to find a quiet place in their everyday environment and take pause from their daily lifestyle to seek and obtain peace. A

Christian should also not forget to add to one's everyday schedule, the word of God, reading and studying the Bible daily. The word of God teaches us the attributes of God and His Son. Daily immersion in the word of God also helps us to live with a better flow of peace. "Follow peace with all men, and holiness, without which no man shall see the Lord." (Hebrews 12:14).

The oppositions to peace are many. Conflict, strife, hostility, and envy all lurk in the shadows, waiting for an opportunity to disrupt your personal peace with the Lord. Before a person became a Christian these were oppositions or disruptions in their life, that kept them from having total peace. Almost everybody seeks peace at some point in life. However, to have peace is not an easy task. Having peace is a lifestyle and an ongoing state of mind. We may all think we have an understanding about peace, but in spite of this, there are so many questions asked about peace. Such as, where can I find peace, how can I obtain peace, can one have total peace, etc. But for one to have peace, the Holy Spirit must be active in that person.

Peace is a self searching word that brings comfort to life. One should seek after peace to allow the spirit of peace to rule in their life individually. Jesus lets us know if we seek after peace we can have peace even in the midst of losing a loved one or during a bitter conflict. For example, for most of us, the passing of a loved one is a very upsetting experience. It is not a good feeling. We all know it is a hurting, disorientating experience as we wonder why it happened. During this time of grief, some people blame themselves, and some people blame others.

All sorts of things run through our mind at the time of bereavement. One must realize that "to everything there is a season, and a time to every purpose under heaven: a time to be born and a time to die..."(Ecclesiastes 3:1-2)

We must pass from this world to be with our Lord and Savior in the next. So while we will grieve the loss of a loved one, we must at the same time take solace(peace) in the fact that life and death are all a part of God's plan. We should also take care to retain our state of peace during the times of conflict. In the heat of conflict, people will say things or do things to another person just to take their mind away from their peace. As Christians we should be representatives of peace to the world through Jesus Christ. After Jesus rose from his death, he found his disciples in a place with the doors shut and locked in fear of the Jews. In the middle of all of this turmoil and confusion, Jesus came and stood in the midst and said "peace be unto you." (John 20: 19).

Anxiety and distress are also opponents of peace. If one's mind is in a state of anxiety, peace is absent within. That means the mind is in a vulnerable state, which can lead to a state of depression. When a person's mind is in an anxious state, it takes away from the normal physical and psychological functioning. Depression can take one's mind so far from reality, that their once familiar surroundings are unrecognizable. Not realizing his/her mind has been taken down this dark path of depression, one may not recognize that the peace and clearness of thought are no longer there. Therefore there is no place of rest or mental peace in that person's mind. One must realize that this is exactly where satan wants our minds to be. The devil is most happy when our minds are in a state of turmoil, distress and conflict. During times of conflict, we are most vulnerable to the devil's efforts to distract our minds from the peace that God intends for man to obtain. That is the peace that Jesus left for all mankind. "And the peace of God which passeth all understanding, shall keep your hearts and minds through Christ Jesus." (Philippians 4:7).

Peace is the Fruit of the Holy Spirit, once a person allows the Holy Spirit to come into their life, peace is at work. All one has to do is cultivate peace because it is already within. No matter what turmoil your mind may have been in before you gave your life to Christ, peace has always been within your being. You can have peace in your mind starting the moment you receive Jesus. Acceptance of Christ means that turmoil, conflict and personal tragedy are in the past now. It's high time to move forward in the Lord. One should have peace in their heart. Peace gives our hearts a certain reassurance that goes beyond our understanding. Peace is of God, we are born of God, peace is already a part of us from the beginning of time. All one has to do is allow peace to surface in their life, and desire to want to continue to have peace as an ongoing lifestyle. Therefore it is up to the individual to want to have peace abide in their life. Once a Christian is awakened to the fact that peace is a part of Christianity, positive thinking goes to work building peace within. We build peace, by going humble before the throne of grace and asking for peace. We must pursue such extraordinary measures in the pursuit of peace, because there is no peace in the world today to be found. Only the peace of God can take away the everyday frustrations and confusion of the mind. "For God is not the author of confusion, but of peace, as in all churches of the Saints." (1 Corinthians 14:33).

🐚 Long Suffering

Long-suffering is showing or having patience in spite of troubles, especially when those troubles are caused by someone else. Going through long-suffering is one of the most difficult times of life. Long-suffering is a part of our daily lives that cannot be eliminated. If we could go through life without the worry and discomfort of long-suffering, Jesus would not have had to die on the cross. Jesus had to endure what he went through because of the fall of Adam and Eve that caused long-suffering to be part of man's nature. Long-suffering is the state of enduring pain, hurt, misery, hardship, and all the turbulence of life. However, because long-suffering is the Fruit of the Holy Spirit, that makes it endurable once a person has repented from all unrighteousness. Long-suffering is a personal endurance, no one can go through another person's long-suffering.

When times become difficult in a person's life one tends to put the blame on others. Sometimes suffering happens because of someone trusting in another person. When one of the persons betrays the trust of another, it can be stressful, and may be called long-suffering. Therefore the one that betrayed the trust has to suffer the consequences of their own actions. The victim suffers because of the betrayal of the trusted one. A good example of trust is marriage, wherein both parties vow to honor the sanctity of their marriage. In cases where these vows are not honored, it is usually the victim who suffers the most. Oftentimes, this suffering is because most of the time the victim didn't know what was going on behind the curtain of on otherwise serene marriage. In this light, we may view betrayal as doing something to another person that could hurt.

Once a person becomes a Christian and opens their heart to Jesus, one can begin to understand the concept of long-suffering. To do this, we must understand the concept of being Christ-like. Some of the virtues Christ embraced are enduring hardship, being strong in all things, and being of good courage. In order to try and approximate these things, we must pray and ask Jesus for understanding. We must be faithful in the Lord. 2 Timothy 2:3 tells us to "endure hardness as a good soldier of Jesus Christ." When people are going through the different adversities of life, it's time to rely and trust in Jesus. Life is always best when we choose to be a Christian. Having Christ in your life makes all the difference in how we are able to handle our adversities. By accepting Jesus in your life you have a close relationship with Him, and you learn how to cast all your cares upon Him. Without the Holy Spirit it is impossible for one to know how to begin to cast all their cares upon Jesus Christ.

We cannot eliminate long-suffering from our lives because it is a part of getting to know Jesus. Sometimes Jesus has to separate us from everything and everyone in our lives to get our attention so we can get closer to Him. "If we suffer, we shall also reign with Him; if we deny Him, he also will deny us." (2 Timothy 2: 12). We do not have to be a Christian to go through adversities in life. "That ye may be the children of your Father which is in heaven: for he maketh his sun to rise on the evil and on the good, and sendeth rain on the just and on the unjust." (Matthew 5:45). In times of need some people turn to Jesus, because he will guide one through one's own adversities. When a person walks through life as a Christian, suffering comes, which builds up character and strength. So why not choose following Jesus as your choice of lifestyle? The best way to get to know how to live for Jesus Christ is by reading the Bible and praying as much as we can throughout the day. These simple activities keep us in touch with the word of God, and the plan of God for our personal life. To get a better understanding of what the Bible is saying, we meditate on the word of God as well as reading His word. Remember when Jesus went to Calvary for man's sins, he was willing and obedient, knowing he had to die for the remission of our sins. It was important to Jesus for mankind to find redemption from sin and become closer to God. Jesus was a perfect example of long-suffering. When we think of the long-suffering that Jesus endured, we know that with Him, we can go through the suffering of this life. We can "do all things through Christ that strengtheneth me." (Philippians 4:13) And indeed we can do all things through Christ, all we have to do is repent of our sins, because Jesus has already done the rest.

🐚 Gentleness

Gentleness is the Fruit of the Holy Spirit. In order to allow gentleness to work in one's life, one has to have a strong mind by the strength of the Holy Spirit. Although there are many people proclaiming their love of Christ, they lack the characteristic of gentleness. Why, because the Fruit of the Holy Spirit is not cultivated in their everyday lifestyle. The Holy Spirit is essential to serving the Lord. Jesus wants to share His gentleness with every human being. In return Jesus wants us to be gentle toward all mankind. Gentleness is knowing salvation is far more important than pride. Instead of arguing to the point of anger, being gentle allows a person to turn away. Turning away shows the courtesy of gentleness, and your example may eventually lead that other person to Christ. A "servant of the Lord must not strive; but be gentle unto all men, apt to teach, patient." (2 Timothy 2:24).

People have the power to influence other people with their speech and actions. A gentle person has a constantly clear mind and is able to recognize the power of influence over others. We must realize that Jesus is in control of all decisions, while remembering that he is not going to force a person to do or say what is right. A person that is gentle already has the mindset to do that which is right in the eyes of Jesus. A person that is gentle will, without wavering, humbly submit to the power of influence, while using the maturity of wisdom that comes from the Grace of God.

While gentleness is giving up the right to make what we think is our own decision, it is building a closer relationship with Jesus. Adam was the first human on the earth: the second Adam is the Lord from heaven. Because humans are influenced to a large extent by what they see in the natural world, people will tend to see with the "natural eye" first. However, the "natural eye" can be deceiving, such that we need a more powerful, all knowing eye to see what we can't see. That is to say, while we use our eyes to see the "natural world," we cannot use our eyes to see the spiritual world. Christians therefore elect to accept Christ as their Savior and follow his guiding eye through this life to help them make the right choices. "I will instruct thee and teach thee in the way which thou shalt go: I will guide thee with mine eye."(Psalm 32:8)

There is a positive to life and a negative to life. Which can be thought of as the breeze and the wind. A soft and gentle breeze can touch many souls, a harsh wind however, can by its hard and forceful fury, destroy much. A gentle mind may be likened to a breeze, it thinks first on things that are positive, no matter what the outcome may be. A not so gentle mind can be likened to a harsh wind, it considers only the negative, regardless of the possibility of a good outcome. Being positive in all things and trusting in the Lord for a positive outcome is what the gentle mind does. "But the wisdom that is from above is first pure, then peaceable, gentle, and easy to be intreated, full of mercy and good fruits, without partiality, and without hypocrisy." (James 3:17).

🌿 Goodness

Goodness is a part of Holiness. It is the Fruit of the Holy Spirit that one should embrace by motivating good and doing good deeds in life. One might ask, how do I motivate good and do good deeds? The answer to that question is that there's only one way to do good continually, and that is through the Holy Spirit. We must first repent of our sins and believe in our hearts that Jesus died for the sins of all mankind. With this belief in place, a person can begin to do what is right in all things. Being good means, (to cite a few examples) to tell the truth all the time, avoidance of strife by closing conflict with the words "let's agree to disagree," treating not only family members with goodness but everybody, being understanding, keeping unity, not stealing, etc. Another method of doing good deeds is the performance of acting upon something that is needed without expecting anything in return. Goodness comes from God. "And Jesus said unto Him, Why callest thou me good? There is none good but one, that is, God." (Mark 10:18).

Jesus wants us to live in truth. Just before he was taken from his disciples, Jesus prayed for the Father to "Sanctify them through thy truth: thy word is truth." (John 17:17). Jesus shows his goodness after the people chose to crucify Him and release Barabbas, the thief. Though they knew of the many good deeds Jesus had done, and what he was capable of doing, the people nevertheless shouted that he should be to crucified. Even as Jesus suffered in agony upon the cross, he was determined to let God's people know the significance of goodness, as he said, "Father, forgive them; for they know not what they do."(Luke 23:34) Although the good and the bad exists side by side in all humans, It is up to each individual to choose which one will rule over their lives. No matter what one chooses it will affect everyone around them in some way. Being good and doing good is always the best choice. It is by the Holy Spirit that a person is able to continue to choose good. A Christian has to grow and practice doing good.

Goodness is Holiness in action. When the Lord elects one to follow Him, one confirms it by repenting and accepting the Holy Spirit. The knowledge of Jesus is all that's necessary to live a godly life. Jesus promised man that he will provide a way of escape from the corruption of this world, if we keep his Commandments. That is the reason Jesus was resurrected from the grave. It is because of His mercies that we are not consumed. "Wherefore also we pray always for you, that our God would count you worthy of this calling, and fulfill all the good pleasure of His goodness, and the work of faith with power." (2 Thessalonians 1:11). So after one puts goodness to action by the power of the Holy Spirit through laboring and suffering without ceasing, you are adopted into the Royal Family of Jesus.

❧ Faith

Faith may be defined as a complete trust of confidence in something or someone. Faith in this context may be thought of as a strong belief in God or religious doctrines based on spiritual belief rather than concrete proof. Faith is something that believers in Christ have even as they have belief that God's will, will be done. Even though we can't "see" faith with our eyes or touch it with our hands, we have faith in God that something may happen or come to pass. This author personally knows of a girl who brought a wedding dress, because the Lord showed her in a dream, that she was walking down the aisle in church, to be married. Prior to having this dream, she didn't have a boyfriend and was not engaged to anyone. She had faith however, that what the Lord showed her in the dream would come to pass. Less than a year later, she was walking down the aisle at church wearing the very dress she had purchased a year prior, to meet her betrothed at the altar and they were wed. It was a beautiful marriage ceremony and the two are still married to this day. This acceptance, based on nothing but faith, of the facts that this lady saw in a dream, demonstrates how we believe in God's messages by means of our faith. Having faith allows the Lord to show us, tell us, and talk to us as individuals. It takes a person's faith to open up their heart and believe God for what he is doing in their life. If a person follows some of the rules of being blessed, faith will follow. Without faith it is impossible to please God.(Hebrews 11:6). Then Jesus went on to tell them, if they had faith they did not need to worry about what they were to eat or drink or what clothes to wear, because their heavenly Father knew what they needed on a daily basis. Jesus said, instead of worrying about these things, one should seek "first the kingdom of God, and his righteousness, and all of these things will be added unto you." (Matthew 6:30-33).

Faith should begin with a Christian walking in the spiritual steps of Christ. However just as a child crawls before it walks, some people have to develop faith over time. Faith is needed in the beginning of a Christian's walk and is necessary in pleasing God. That means that after a person becomes a Christian, faith is a part of that person's life. Once a person begins to walk in Christ, one is able to build on faith and hope. Faith is the idea of being able to establish a strong belief of things we cannot see. Spiritual substance is the root idea of standing with the claim of faith, and hope is God's promise. To all who believe, righteousness is given to us by faith in Jesus Christ. Faith is also a necessity as we work towards making it to the kingdom of God to hear the words "well done" because you were a good and faithful servant.

It is important for a Christian to allow the Holy Spirit to lead and show them how faith works. Regarding faith, the Bible says, "Now faith is the substance of things hoped for, the evidence of things not seen." (Hebrews 11:1). If we take those words from the Bible and learn what they mean, we will understand what faith is. Looking at the words "hoped for," and "not seen," in this context, can be better understood by considering the following. If one is lacking the stability with the knees and needs a cane or a walker to obtain stability, that person is walking with the HOPE of not falling. But the person cannot actually "SEE" his FAITH in the cane or walker, he has to believe it will work, and that's where the belief in something "not seen" comes into play. As one believes in faith by the Holy Spirit that dwells on the inside, (standing by faith that one's knees will continue to hold them up and not buckle) that is the evidence not seen. Jesus keeps man even when they're not aware. Faith without works is dead. (James 2:14-26). Christians have to keep the faith in times of adversity, by standing up to whatever trying situation comes along. Sometimes a person may feel that calling on

Jesus for a particular situation is of no use, and no one else seems to care. Trying times, overwhelming stress, and conflict are the times when that person needs Jesus the most. A Christian cannot forget about the faith that's in them by the Holy Spirit. Jesus is standing there, for those with faith, waiting, ready to help, whenever a Christian calls his name, and to help to overcome whatever a person asks. He wants us to ask for his help at any time. And what makes our relationship with Jesus so much more beautiful, is that he knows what you need before you even venture to ask. Sometimes situations in life can be so overwhelming such that one may feel like giving up on the faith. It is at these times, that it is most important to remember to build up your faith. Take a stand on those prayers you have already laid up before God when things were going good in life. Disappointment will come, and if we live long enough we will have some problems that we cannot solve. Know that while walking down those rocky roads in life, that all problem solving is in our Lord Jesus Christ

🌾 Meekness

Meekness is the Fruit of the Holy Spirit. Once a person has repented of their sins and become a Christian, it's time to begin to seek after meekness. To be meek one must first rely on the Holy Spirit for guidance. Because without guidance of the Holy Spirit, true meekness can not exist. Human nature dictates that even the most pious of people will not be able to truly continue being submissive toward one another, or humble themselves or "turn the other cheek" when it's necessary without the Holy Spirit working in their life. Meek is a small word with lots of power. And that power is needed for the work of (people) Christians that truly want to walk with Jesus. A person has to walk worthy to one's own calling with all "lowliness and meekness, with long suffering, forbearing one another in love." (Ephesians 4:1-3) Christians must endeavor to keep the unity of the Spirit in the bond of peace. Meekness in one's life comes through the Holy Spirit. Meekness also predisposes us to have love toward one another as well.

When a person turns away from worldly ways and begins to walk with Jesus, the lust of the eye, the pride of life and the lust of the flesh all fall away as the autumn leaves fall from a tree. Walking with Jesus allows all of these sinful and wicked things to pass away from that person. It's time to stand up and follow after righteousness, and the things that are of God, such as having faith, love, being patient, humble and meek. A meek person should always be ready to do whatever is good, have peace and be gentle toward everybody.

🌿 Temperance

Things such as temperance-moderation or self-restraint; self-control; abstinence from alcoholic liquors or sex, can be contained by the Holy Spirit. Abstinence is the act or practice of refraining from indulging an appetite or desire of the flesh. Abstinence also helps a person concentrate on the Holy Spirit by suppressing the desires of the flesh. Temperance is the fruit of the Holy Spirit that provides Christians with the power to resist temptation. It gives a person self-control, self-discipline, self-denial, and the strength to refrain from the things that are not of God. Just because one has professed the Holy Spirit, doesn't mean that person has temperance. Acquiring temperance-moderation takes practice. Christians have to learn how to have self-control, self-discipline, self-denial, and how to refrain from and resist the worldly temptations we encounter in daily life. One cannot have temperance without repentance of one's sins. After repentance, one has to accept the Holy Spirit as the choice of leadership and Lord over one's life.

Christians demonstrate temperance by self-control. The powers of darkness are forever present around us, and one must remember that Jesus is the only one who can overcome these powers. Without having Jesus in one's life, it is impossible to obtain a constant life of self-control. The powers of darkness are anything that can destroy humanity. "And Jesus came and spake unto them, saying, All power is given unto me in heaven and in earth." (Matthew 28:18). Once a Christian becomes aware of who and where power comes from, one can begin to work on one's self-control. One must have self-discipline. "Study to show thyself approved unto God...".(See 2 Timothy 2:15) Why? Because if one doesn't meditate on the word of God, one will indulge in things that are not godly, sometimes unaware. The Holy Spirit will allow a person to deny things that are not of God when all else seems hopeless. The Holy Spirit gives one the strength to deny things that are unacceptable to Jesus such as, alcoholism, drug use, adultery or other sexual activities that are ungodly, over eating or just saying "no" to people. One has to make up one's own mind to follow Jesus. Following Jesus, means accepting the fact that it is not MY will Lord, but YOUR will that will be done in my life.

A Christian has to give control over to Jesus by giving Him their thoughts (mind), body and soul. Giving control to Jesus can be done through prayer, and by reading and studying the word of God. Studying the word of God is also how one learns the attributes of God. Studying God's word allows one to know and understand what Jesus expects from a Christian. Give Jesus control over one's tongue because "the tongue can no man tame; it is an unruly evil, full of deadly poison." (James 3:8). Anger, however, is something man has no control over without the help of the Holy Spirit. If one wants to control anger, simply surrender it to the Holy Spirit, and it will be done. What makes most hold onto anger is the desire to get revenge over someone else. Jesus said, vengeance is mine, He will repay. Therefore if Christian's give their anger to Jesus, He said He would take care of the situation.

WHAT IS LOVE?

*I*n considering the nature of love, one might question, how do we know when we are in love with another person? How does one know if another person loves them? Does one love another person for who that person is or does one love another for the material advantages or financial resources that the other person may have? Wikipedia says, love is a variety of different feelings, states, and attitudes that range from interpersonal affection("I love my mother") to pleasure ("I love that meal"). The word "love" can refer to a strong emotional attachment to something or someone, or a strong personal attachment to something or someone.

According to Hebrews 13:1 we are to "let brotherly love continue." That means we should exercise human kindness, compassion, affection, and the unselfish loyal benevolent concern for the good of another. What men say love is, and what God says love is, are two different things. Jesus said he wants us to love one another as we love ourselves (See Matthew 22:39). Is loving another as we love ourselves possible in today's world? What did Jesus mean by love another person as you love yourself? When we sing, "Oh, how I love Jesus, because He first loved me," we realize it's a problem with some humans to love someone who does not love them back. There are many of us walking around day after day thinking we know what love is, but the sad truth is that many of us do not know what love is. If you love someone, why would you mistreat them by being verbally, physically, mentally, spiritually or sexually abusive? Before and even during his crucifixion, Jesus was abused in every way possible, "As many were astounded at thee; his visage was so marred more than any man, and his form more than the sons of men." (Isaiah 52:14) In Reading Isaiah 52:14, and other scriptures,(See Luke 23:33-43, Mark 15:25-39, etc.), we are reminded of how Jesus was beaten, humiliated and then crucified in a manner that was especially cruel even by Roman standards of the day. Would they have treated Him that way if they loved Him? They asked Him why he didn't call on his God, the father, they taunted and verbally abused Him by calling Him the King of the Jews, etc. He was abused mentally while he was hanging on the cross, and in anguish cried out: "My God, my God, why hast thou forsaken me?"(Matthew 27:46) More verbal, mental and Spiritual abuse followed when they kept telling Him, He was not the son of God, He was a blasphemer, and if He was the son of God to come down from the cross. (See Matthew 27:40). Why did Jesus tolerate this abusive treatment? Because He loves mankind and his purpose was to show this love by sacrificing himself. No one forced Him to sacrifice himself, He did it because His concern was getting man redeemed back to God.

One of the purposes of the 10 Commandments is to teach us to love God above all. It starts out with "thou shalt have no other gods before Me."(Exodus 20:3). In other words, God wants humans to put Him first and foremost in our everyday life. God further commands that no representative images of deities be made and worshiped. We are commanded to honor our father and mother. One of the ways we can honor our parents is to obey them "in the Lord, for this is right."(See Ephesians 6:1) Honoring our parents is what we call Philos Love or friendship love, and family love. Thou shalt not steal, thou shalt not kill, thou shalt not commit adultery, etc. These are a few of the more well known Commandments that are commonly ignored in our world today. Other commandments that are more serious in nature are also commonly ignored, such as murder. Murder, commonly known as homicide, is talked about, written about and is the subject of much curiosity of many otherwise educated people. The words, "Thou shalt not kill," seem to be as empty as the wind in today's world. Murder/mayhem and murder oriented themes seem to be almost glorified in an endless stream of computer games, tabloid and newspaper articles, news reports and motion pictures. Why do people seem so fascinated with the concept of taking the life of another? Does this fascination with murder find its roots in the individual's loss of direction on the path to Jesus or do some people allow satan to blind them to the fact that murder is wrong? Murder is surely NOT what Jesus meant when he said we should love one another. When faced with the many moral dilemmas satan will put in your way, reading the Bible daily and meditating on God's word gives the Christian the spiritual strength he needs to repel satan's suggestions and advances.

People are not only stealing from their immediate neighbors, but today computers have given people the ability to steal from strangers. Adultery and sexual perversions are the subject of many prime time talk shows. People will often tell unflattering lies about their neighbors and friends, and in spite of the commandment that it not be so, openly desire the material things, etc., that their neighbor may have. (See Exodus 20:1-17). After While Moses wrote the 10 Commandments given to Him by God, many other Commandments were made. We cannot know for certain if these additional commandments were from God or made by man. Some people don't believe we should follow the 10 Commandments. Other people don't know what to believe regarding the 10 Commandments and others don't believe in following anything.

As Christians we should learn how to get in touch with our inner self. Receiving the Holy Spirit, is how we learn to get in touch with our inner self. Without being in tune with our inner self, we are out of control. Although we think we can control ourselves, the temptations of this world present many obstacles to salvation. We think, in our arrogance, that we can control ourselves, but it is impossible without the guidance of the Holy Spirit, that dwells within us all. The Holy Spirit is the love from the breath of life we all have within us. The sooner man understands Love is the breath of life, the sooner man will understand Love is the key through life. We think we can, but we cannot control what goes on in our lives. We only think we are in control of ourselves and what goes on within our lives, but God gave all control to Jesus. Jesus has everything in control as He sees and knows all things. There are obstacles set before us throughout life. We should be aware that we should be mindful in everything we do, or say, and how it is said, as failure to do so opens the door to satan's influence. Once we come into the knowledge of Christ's Resurrection we learn the works of satan. In everybody there's some positive and negative. Love helps us to abstain from doing and speaking what's negative toward one another, and helps us do what is positive. We were born with a portion of love. We are also born into sin. Because we were born into sin, Jesus came and bore our sins in his body on the cross, so that we could live into righteousness. (See 1 Peter 2:24). In reviewing Christ's life, every point of view highlights the fact that if he wasn't who he was, i.e., the Son of God, he wouldn't have been able to withstand what he had to endure. But because Jesus was the Son of God, and therefore knew God's purpose and plan, He had to withstand what he knew was his destiny, for the redemption of mankind. (See Matthew 27:27-37) In retrospect, we can see that it was love that gave Him the strength and energy to persevere. Jesus suffered and endured much so that we would know that it is possible to stand up against any evil that is put before us. By living according to the word of God, we can conquer any negative thoughts that enter our minds. Just to say "I love you" to someone is not enough. If you truly love someone, those words must be followed up with an active program of consideration and affection. Jesus came to show mankind that we should love one another as we love ourselves. Loving and actively displaying love in our daily activities is what Jesus wants us to do most of all. If we love one another, in the manner that Jesus wants us to, one will find that the love of God is dwelling on the inside of us all. Without God there is no love. God's love continues to forgive us no matter if we're right or wrong.

We are all God's children, and as God loves us, so should we have a love for our children. Abuse is not a part of love. If you say you love God, abuse should not be in your outlook, even though you know it's going on elsewhere. There are countless numbers of children, husbands, wives, cousins, nieces, nephews, friends, aunts, and uncles, who suffer abuse on a daily basis. Abusers will often say they love those they abuse, however, where there is abuse there is no love. When you love someone you don't keep hurting them. Psalms 63:3-4 says, "because thy loving kindness is better than life, my lips shall praise thee. I will bless thee while I live: I will lift up my hands in thy name." God created us in his likeness, that's why we are born with a portion of love. It is up to you to cultivate the portion of love God has given you in the beginning of your life. It is up to the individual to kindle and nourish the love God has given us through Jesus by the Holy Spirit.

We are governed by spirits in the atmosphere, whether it be by the Holy Spirit or community spirits. The Bible labels Community spirits as "principalities and powers of the air." Every human being has a natural, spiritual, and physical aspect of their nature. Think of it this way: initially, man came from the dust, that's the "natural" aspect of human nature. Secondly, God blew the breath of life into man, that's the "spiritual" aspect of human nature. And after the breath of life, man became a living being, that's the "physical" aspect of human nature. Afterwards, God gave man a mind such that he could think for himself, a body as a temple to keep Holy, and a soul to give back to Him. God is in control at all times, however, He allows man to make his own decisions. "For as many are led by the Spirit of God, they are the sons of God" (Romans 8:14). It's up to the individual to choose which influences he will allow to rule his life. Sometimes even though we have love in our hearts, we are condemned by the things we do, especially when we know we're not doing the will of God. There is no way we can love someone and yet hate them in the same breath. Either you will love the one and hate the other. Ye cannot serve God and mammon. (See Matthew 6:24) Loving the one and hating the other is where the governing over one's mind, body, and soul take preference. Who do you choose to be Lord over your life?

🖌 Love Conquers All

True love conquers all, but some would rather go to therapy to solve their love related problems. In further pursuit of solving love related issues, some will go to a psychiatrist, while others may pursue some type of short term counseling. Others will not seek any kind of solutions to their love related problems, because that's just the way life is for them. It's hard for a carnal mind to understand the true essence of what love truly means because "the carnal mind is enmity against God."(See Romans 8:7). Some say that love is merely an emotion, therefore if love is an emotion, then God must have emotion. There is a difference between God's emotions and man's emotions. The difference is man's emotions are unstable, God's emotion is the same all the time. In light of God's emotion, consider the Scripture that tells us "then Jesus wept." (See John 11:35). Even though Jesus was sent directly from heaven by God and took upon Himself a man's body, and by so doing, subjected himself to being able to experience human emotion. The act of volunteering to experience human emotion tells us God has emotions. When we talk about the emotions of man we are speaking of ups and downs. We may hear the words, "I love you today, but I don't know if I'll love you tomorrow," meaning that it all depends on how one feels from day to day. So when you look at love in the sense of emotions, one must keep in mind that there are ups and downs in the eyes and ways of man.

The essence of true love is mutual trust and respect towards one another. Love is having compassion eternal and enduring though all things. Love is kindness, love is patience, love is innocence, love never seeks revenge and love is also saying, I'm sorry. If we have Jesus in our life, loving and being loved is not a hard task. Love is also wisdom, forgiveness and keeping fear out of one's inner self. As a Christian, giving and accepting love from another person is important. There is a measure of love in all of our hearts. We know this because everybody seeks love, hoping that when they find it, that person will love them back. When one is looking for love without Jesus, how does one know if the love that may be found is genuine? Children probably need love most of all, because a child can wither and die (due to failure to thrive,) which comes in part from lack of love. With the understanding that we are born with a measure of love, we should accept love as being a part of our everyday lives. Love should be shown from person to person, as well as received from person to person. If we know Jesus, we know what it means to Him for us to love one another, and to love everybody unconditionally. Sometimes we have to go through a trial or experience something unpleasant before we realize the magnitude of the love that God has for us. "For God so loved the world that he gave his only begotten son..." (See John 3:16).

LOVE AMONG FAMILY
AND FRIENDS

*L*ove is not always as it appears, and as individuals we experience love in many different ways. Take for instance, a typical husband and wife, who appear to be the very epitome of marital bliss and happiness when they are in public. To all outward appearances, it seems as though the love they have for each other is boundless. However, once out of the public eye at home, they can't say a kind word to each other. When they are speaking to each other, they are frequently arguing and bickering, seemingly oblivious to fact that their children are listening to every harsh word and watching their every move. In their zeal to hurt each other, this couple doesn't realize they're hurting their children more than ourselves. In fact, by presenting an otherwise outward appearance of marital bliss and happiness, they are living a lie, and indirectly, teaching their children how to live and lie in this manner. This couple is in effect, showing their children how to live a "double life by deceit," that they will probably imitate in their adult lives. Perpetrating this type of behavior in our daily lives comes from not paying attention to the voice of God. Not hearing God's voice and following his commands are one of the many ways we allow satan to infiltrate the atmosphere of our homes, our jobs, and our everyday life. Not paying attention to God's voice makes us double minded and unstable. "If any of you lack wisdom, let him ask of God.. But let him ask in faith, nothing wavering. For he that wavereth is like a wave of the sea..Let not that man think he shall receive any thing of the Lord.. A double minded man is unstable in all his ways." (see James 1:5-8) True love does not exclude our children, as our children are a part of the family unit and we as parents should respect them as such. We [adults] are examples to children in every way, especially when it comes to showing them love. In Jeremiah 31:3, we read that the people didn't think the Lord was as good to them as he used to be, however the Lord tells the people that his love for them is the same, and eternally unchanging. Jeremiah 31:3 ends with the words, "with loving kindness have I drawn thee." And with this in mind, we should draw others as well as our children and anyone else we come in contact with the same loving kindness. God gave children and parents a charge towards one another by saying, "children obey your parents in the Lord: for this is right." (See Ephesians 6:1), God further instructs fathers to not provoke their children to anger(See Ephesians 6:4.) God wants us to love each other, not fight, or see who can yell the loudest or who can become the most incensed. God first loved us and showed his love by sending Jesus

[His only Son] down from heaven for the salvation of all mankind. We can't buy love, we can't steal love, and we can't borrow love. We can only achieve God's love through Jesus. God further instructs us that not only are we to love our children, but we are to love everybody.

Raising Children

- If we disapprove of our children by shortcomings, our children learn to blame.
- If we are argumentative to others, our children learn hostility
- If our children are around humiliation, they may lose self respect
- If we degrade our children, that brings about shyness
- If a child is criticized, He/She learns to find fault
- If a child's environment is permissive He/She gains knowledge of endurance
- If children are encouraged they gain knowledge of confidence
- If children are taught freedom they gain independence
- If a child's environment is impartial they gain knowledge of honesty

I read a poem in a book ("Siblings." See page 37, "Tears and joys of Life," by Velow) which spoke of a child who went to school one day hungry. This child had not eaten because her mother's mind had slipped away after the passing of the children's father. The mother was not able to function, not even so much as to feed her own children. When the child got in the lunch line to get lunch one day, she took a few bites of the food, and put the rest in her pocket for her siblings, who were not old enough to go to school. After reading the poem, I thought about how sometimes parents will unknowingly mistreat their children because something happened, (that they blamed on the child, or that the child was the cause of) that changed the whole course of their lifestyle. The effect of changing lifestyles was so profound that the parents found it hard to cope with this "new" life style that had been "forced" on them. During the time that the parent is trying to adjust to this new lifestyle, the parent is not mentally, physically, emotionally or cognitively able to meet the needs of their children. Those of us that are raised in a Christian home, do not realize how privileged it is to come from a Christian environment. Proverbs 22:6 tells us to train up our children in the way they should go and when they get old, the training will always be with them. However, in spite of influences to the contrary, not all children follow the ways of their upbringing. In cases where the child seems to be going astray, we must use the love we have for our children, and the love they have for us, to gently bring them back into the fold. We bring our children closer to us, by love through Jesus Christ. Without the guidance of love, satan will have us thinking we're doing right by our children, (or anything else,) when in actuality he[satan] has taken over our lives and we don't realize what is going on. We must always be aware that satan is constantly roaming the earth seeking whom ever he can devour. (See 1 Peter 5:8). When we study the Bible and live according to the principles contained therein, we find that we are more than capable of coping with the challenges (be they spiritual or otherwise) that we encounter on a daily basis. It is important for parents and all adults to take special care to be the example Jesus wants us to be around our children. That means making sure that as Christians, we spend quality time with our children praying and reading the Bible. This quality time is necessary so they can understand not only how to love and share love, "but by love to serve one another." (See Galatians 5:13). When Christian parents are not living a Christ like life, not only do the children notice this contradiction, but others notice it as well. Most children look up to adults as role models. These role models can take the form of a parent, teacher, preacher or any other adult. We as role models most therefore be careful that our influence in our children's life is positive and not negative. As Christians learning what love is, and how to continue to love without fail, is to be a part of our everyday life. We show our love by being true to the children around us in spirit, deed and truth, no matter where we are or what role we play in a child's life.

Families are where we connect ourselves and share the experiences of past, present, and future generations. In the family setting, one can experience stories of triumphs and disappointments, happiness and sadness, support and let downs, cheers and "boos", loyalty and fraternity and most of all love. Family by the word of God is to "bear one another's burdens," (See Galatians 6:2) be strong for one another and understand that no matter what the problem, by uniting together in love, we can stand. God made us all different, no two people have the same fingerprints, not even twins. Spiritually everybody comes into this world as one individual and leaves as one individual. But on the other hand, once we enter this world we are never alone. God did not intend for man to be alone. We can see this desire to not be alone in instances where a person, having been separated from their biological family (for whatever reason,) will spend a great deal of time and energy trying to find their biological family later in life. Others are content, having bonded with the family that raised them, to stay with this family, in lieu of the pursuit of their actual biological relatives. The underlying principle here is that everybody needs somebody.

Being a family member however, has responsibilities, expectations and obligations. We have a responsibility towards loyalty, honesty and sharing as a family member. These qualities are also expected in a friendship. In order to help our children grow up to be responsible citizens, parents have a responsibility to provide for their children's needs in this physical world as well as their spiritual well being. We as Christians are expected to stand firm in the word of God, believe the word, be a doer of the word, and most of all love everybody even as Christ loves us. Jesus told us if we love Him we will keep His commandments. (See John 14:15). Some of us think that keeping His commandments is a hard task because we're not in tune with ourselves as individuals. Jesus tells us to "come unto me, all ye that labour and are heavy laden.. take my yoke upon you and learn of me... For my yoke is easy, and my burden is light." (See Matthew 11:28-30) In spite of Jesus inviting us to come unto Him, we have so many reasons and excuses why we can't follow His will. For instance, I have heard people say, "every time I try to love someone it hurts" or "I just can't get along with my mother, I love her but we don't see eye to eye about most things, my teenager won't listen, my mom doesn't care about me or my siblings, we(relatives, etc.,) never have gotten along, they(parents, etc.,) were never there for us," ad infinitum. Overcoming these obstacles may seem like a daunting task, but all we have to do is come unto Jesus, and these burdens will be lifted.

Now let's talk talk some more about Philos Love, which is the love close friends have for each other. Philos Love is supposed to be the special love one has for another person besides their significant other. Love is not always a two-way street. To state once again, we sing the song, "Oh, how I love Jesus, because He first loved me," but do we really appreciate what that means? We were created by love, "He that loveth not knoweth not God: for God is love." (1 John 4:8). For that reason all men are born with love. However some of us abuse love towards one another. We can say we love someone all day with our mouth, but love is showing someone that you love them with kind deeds as well as with kind words. When we say we love someone that should mean "I will follow you to the end". A friendship type of love is like brotherly love. As long as you stay with Christ, there should be nothing you wouldn't do for your loved one. Follow my example, as I follow the example of Christ. (See 1 Corinthians 11:1). Love is being kind, truthful, and understanding. Is there a dark side of love? No, Love doesn't have a dark side, sure there will be some ups and downs and satan would like us to think there is no way out. Satan (the adversary) is walking to and fro the earth seeking whom he may devour. (See 1 Peter 5:8). So, satan will do whatever he can to distract or take your mind from the love of God. Don't think you can ever relax and drop your guard, because, satan (the adversary) will never cease his endeavors. If he doesn't take your mind off of God the first time, he will be back at a later date and try again. Resisting satan's distractions and obstacles is a never ending battle as long as we're fighting for the kingdom of heaven. Satan's interference can be seen especially in family or friendship disagreements. If the parties involved do not have their minds on God, satan will use this lapse of devotion and have the whole family and/or friendship/relationships in disarray.

Is there a dark side to God? There isn't a dark side to God but there is a dark side to man. Why? God made us in his own image (See Genesis 1:27), and blew his breath into man and man became a living soul. (See Genesis 2:7). Love is the light that shines on man. The love in mankind is the joy, peace, long-suffering, gentleness, goodness, faith, meekness, and temperance that keeps the light shining. Just as the serpent told Eve she shall not surely die if she eats of the forbidden tree in the garden of Eden, (See Genesis 3:3-5). satan will surely do all he can to get man to taste of whatever the forbidden fruit of his tree is today. To taste of the fruit of satan's tree however, one has to caste aside the light of love and adopt the darkness of sin. Reading the Bible daily is one of the ways a Christian resists adopting satan's darkness. Because we realize that the light of God's word obliterates the darkness of sin, we as Christians, need to get out in our community as well as circulate among our family and friends and spread the word of love in the name of Jesus, and let one another know we don't have to live in the darkness of sin. There are so many people who misunderstand what the word love really means. Some of us don't know the origin of the word love. God is love. (See 1 John 4:8). In this verse, John is telling us that if a person does not know God, he does not love, because God is love. God created man in his own image, however, Jesus was on the scene at the beginning of time, and still stands before all men today.

🌸 Has love changed?

God intimately engaged Himself with his creation when he breathed the breath of life into Adam. The Bible says God never changes, "For I am The Lord, I change not…"(See Malachi 3:6). We know God (Our Creator) as a God of justice, one who loves righteousness, hates wickedness, feels anger and is compassionate. God, in the role of a father has compassion on his children(mankind), so the Lord has compassion on those who fear Him(See Psalm 103:13); We know God as a God of joy and laughter. God however, doesn't laugh in the manner in which a man laughs. The Lord laughs at the wicked, for He knows their day is coming. (see Psalm 37:13) Humans also respond to those same expressions. We are made in the image of God. Is God emotional? Through Jesus we know God has a passionate side. Although God loves us infinitely he is not pleased by our rebellion against Him. Does this mean our emotions are the same as God's? The answer is "no," because God cannot sin, but because of man's sinful nature man's emotions are corrupt, and therefore man can sin. "For from within, out of the heart of men, proceed evil thoughts, adulteries, fornications, murders, thefts, covetousness, wickedness, deceit, lasciviousness, an evil eye, blasphemy, pride, foolishness: All these evil things come from within, and defile the man."(Mark 7:21-23) When God gets angry there is no malice, it is divine and therefore the consequences are divine justice, unaffected by emotion. When man commits vengeful or vicious acts, it's often fueled by anger. Man's anger is volatile and subject to get out of control because of his sinful nature. All of God's emotions are within his divine nature and expressed without sin. The Old Testament tells us so much about God's love toward us. "The Lord is good to all: and his tender mercies are over all his works."(Psalm 145:9) Man was tricked into sin. Even though God told Adam and Eve not to eat of the tree of knowledge, and they did it anyway, God did not forsake man and yield Adam and Eve to satan. God had a plan for man's salvation, and that plan was in the form of Jesus, our redeemer. Jesus is no longer here on earth in the flesh, but, if we only believe, we will find him with us in love and in the Spirit. Because of our sinful nature, our sincerity and credibility has gotten progressively thin over the generations. Without the Holy Spirit and the love of God, we cannot be loyal to one another and truly love one another as God intended. God never intended for us to have a bad day, every day with God is a good day. Yes, we will have some days that are disappointing, days when things don't go the way we think they should, even crazy days, but there is something good in every day, even if it's just the fact that we woke up. Let's thank God for Jesus, for therein lies the hope that we have another chance to love and another day to get closer to Him. We don't understand what we're missing when we don't have the love of God in charge of our lives. Peter told us to cast all of our cares upon God for he cares for us. (See 1 Peter 5:7) In other words, he loves us and will carry our burdens, be they spiritual or emotional. God doesn't want you to worry about anything--nothing at all. When we put our problems in our own hands and try to figure out how to solve them ourselves, we're saying "no" to God's judgment and "no" to Jesus as well. Our human arrogance is saying: "I can handle this, I can take care of this situation myself." When we fail to resolve our problem in this manner, we become emotionally upset and wonder why things didn't work out on our behalf. That's another response of our physical-mental nature, which is called emotion, and this response is hard to let go. The more we choose to let God's love abide in us the easier it is to let go of our flawed emotional responses. The Bible tells us in John 15:7, If the word of God abides in us and we abide in the word of God, we can ask anything in the name of Jesus and it will be done unto us. "Herein is My father glorified, that ye bear much fruit; so shall ye be my disciples."(John 15:8) We abide in God's word that gives us the fruit we need to bear whatever is set before us in our walk of life. If you get a job and don't go to work, you can't expect to receive a paycheck. Without a job, you will find yourself without money, and not able to pay your bills. Likewise, when we walk with Jesus, we have a spiritual job, and if we don't "work" on our spiritual job, we can't expect to reap our "spiritual paycheck." When we walk with Jesus we are seeking not only the promise of spiritual reward, but the promise of eternal life with Christ as well. We do this by prayer and supplication in love, which is literally a request or petition.(See Philippians 4:6-14). Christians really ought to pray every day to get closer to Jesus, learn about the love He has for us to sustain the love of God. Is it necessary? Yes it is, consider how much quality time we spend with our loved ones each day. Jesus requires quality time each day also, and in this way we further our relationship with Him. We are in a war every day against the satan's dark legions that would not only cut us off from Jesus, but cut us off from God as well. "For we wrestle not against flesh and blood, but against principalities, against powers, against the rulers of darkness of this world, against spiritual wickedness in high places."(Ephesians 6:12) Jesus needs us to spend quality time with Him in the same manner in which we spend quality time with those of our inner circle. Jesus tells us in a parable that man ought always to pray and not faint.(See Luke 18:1) Jesus is telling us that no matter what obstacles come our way, we should pray. We should pray, no matter how tough times are, no matter how bad we think our day is going, we should pray, no matter what the situation or circumstance. We should pray, and in so doing, we are casting our cares upon Jesus. Even if Jesus doesn't come when we think He should, we have to believe and be rest assured that he will come in due time. Jesus' love for us is the key to God's heart. In human affairs, we know that the more you are around your loved one and enjoying them, the more you want to be around them. It's the same with Jesus, the more you pray and cry out to Him, the MORE you want to pray and cry out to Him. Why, because when you pray with a sincere heart Jesus shows up with his love and it spills over into your soul which causes the joy of the Lord to over flow and strengthen you in all things. After so many times of His joy overflowing into your soul, it is so much love that you can't help but to share it with everyone you know, including your enemies. Praying and crying out to Jesus is how we get to know the love that Jesus came down to spread abroad and share with all mankind. Basking in the love Jesus gave to mankind is another benefit of getting to know God through Jesus.

❦ Has Love Changed?

Has love changed? The Bible says, "Let love be without dissimulation. Abhor that which is evil, cleave to that which is good." (Romans 12:9-21) Meaning, it doesn't matter what color a person's skin is, how they look, and any disabilities they may have such as blindness, impaired speech, paraplegia or anything that we can't agree with in our own minds, we are supposed to love unconditionally. How a person looks or acts is nobody's business but that person and God's. We are NOT accountable for the actions or thoughts of others. We are however, accountable for our OWN actions and thoughts as individuals. Our first impression of another person is usually based on little or no objective evidence. Instead of trying to evaluate a person by first impressions, our hearts and our minds should be on greeting them with the love of Jesus. Greeting someone with the love of Jesus can take the form of a short few words. Greeting with the love of Jesus gives us a chance to show love towards that person even though we do not know who they are. We can not know the battles that a person may be fighting in their lives, but showing love to that person might be all that person needs to help them overcome a personal situation and continue with their day. In some respects, it is sometimes much easier speaking and talking to someone you do not know, than it is speaking and talking to someone you do know. Speaking with anyone, whether you know them or not is all about the love of Jesus which is showing hospitality, charity and love. When Christians see someone in obvious distress on the streets, we should love the person and not judge their condition. We should look beyond that homeless person's condition, we should look beyond the plight of the drug addict or alcoholic, or any other disorder a person may have and show them love. People with afflictions and conditions are people also and they need Jesus just as well as the next person that looks like what we call "normal." A Christian's first impression to a stranger should be acceptable to Christ, meaning do what Jesus told us to do. In the Bible, Jesus said if they're hungry give them food, thirsty give them something to drink. (See Matthew 25:35) The Bible also commands us to welcome one another as Christ welcomed you, for the glory of God.(See Romans 15:7) The Bible also instructs us to let brotherly love continue, to show hospitality to strangers, because some have entertained Angels unaware. (See Hebrews 13:1-3) If we truly want to be set free from satan's influences, one of the many things we can do is love unconditionally with a smile, because the joy of the Lord is our strength.

PRESS ON

I feel so tired but, I gotta keep pressing
I feel like giving up but, I don't wanna miss my blessing
I gave it to the Lord, why am I stressing
I guess this is where I suppose to use my weapon
I got my Helmet, my sword, my shield for protection
With the love of God I know I can't lose my direction
—*Durand Huggins*

GOD'S WAY OF LOVE

*W*hen most of us are young we seek love. Although people come into and go out of our lives (for whatever reason), we continue to seek love. As time passes, we realize just because we feel love for someone and they say they feel the same love toward us, this love is not always true love and it usually doesn't last forever. Sometimes we think we are so much in love with a person, we allow them to abuse us in so many ways. We think that if we just hold on a little longer things will change. We make these accommodations because everything is new to us as young adults, and we think the abuse will stop and love will flourish. We don't have enough life experience as young adults to know that the object of our love and affections will probably never be the person we hoped he or she would be. There are all types and forms of what many dare to label as "love." In some cases" love" is really a form of abuse. A few examples of this so-called "love" may take the form of mental, physical, sexual, and even spiritual abuse. Is this abusive form of "love," the love that God means that we should have for one another? In contemplating this question, remember we are talking about how God wants us to love each other. Abuse is not something that is strictly confined to an interaction between two people. A person can, for example, indulge in self abuse. Self abuse can be accomplished in many ways, but some of the more prevalent examples of self abuse are the use of illegal drugs, or alcohol. Abuse in all of its forms does not usually overcome a person in "one fell swoop," it usually starts off in many small ways. Abuse or abusive situations do, however, usually get worse with time. After a pattern of abuse has been in your life for a long time, it's hard to adopt a new life style to get out of or away from it. In spite of the fact that something or someone is abusive to us, it may still be hard to walk away from the situation. Most of us know of, or have heard of someone who has been in an abusive situation as either the victim or the perpetrator, and suffered horribly as a result of what was supposed to have been a loving relationship. Abuse may be seen in all types of relationships, such as, husbands being abusive to their wives, and wives being abusive to their husbands, parents to their children, children to parents, siblings to siblings, girlfriends, boyfriends, and Christians abusing Christians. The question is, where is the love in this type of lifestyle? Is there truly a dark side of love?

When a person proclaims himself to be a Christian, there are certain standards that he is expected to live up to, such as living a Christ like life style in his daily interactions with other people. Another one of those standards concerns loving and showing love in the manner that Christ showed love to mankind. When we talk about love as a Christian, it is with the understanding that love is a certain outstanding part of our everyday lifestyle. In furtherance of this loving lifestyle, Christians should walk around with love in their hearts and on their minds throughout the day, with love being uppermost in our innermost thoughts. Furthermore, as Christians, we must follow Christ's example and remember that love should be with us twenty-four hours a day, seven days a week. The Bible tells us that "God so loved the world that he gave his only begotten son.." (See John 3: 16). So just imagine why did God gave his only begotten son? Why was Jesus' sacrifice necessary? I'll say, Jesus' sacrifice was necessary because of man's fall from grace. Although man was God's creation and made in His own image,(See Genesis 1:27) man had fallen away from God's will(grace). In order for man to get back to God, mankind needed a redeemer, and that redeemer was in the form of Jesus Christ, God's son.

Love is not always what it appears, and we all experience love in so many different ways. We may examine the case of (as mentioned earlier), a husband and wife who may give the appearance that makes people think they're so much in love with each other. However, when this same "loving" couple gets home, they can't stop degrading each other in front of their children. I'm talking about Christians with children looking and listening to their every move and word. Honest people don't deceive one another. We allow these things to come into our lives because we are not paying attention to what God's will is for our lives. If we love God we will keep his commandments and His commandments are not grievous (See 1 John 5:3). Not paying attention to, or otherwise not keeping God's commandments, is how satan comes in and infiltrates the prayerful atmosphere in our homes and lives. Allowing satan's influence to run rampant in our homes and in our lives, throws our minds off the track of the will of God as a family, a couple and as an individual. It is important for a Christian family to find quality time with the Lord together as one, and on an individual basis, show love toward God and each other. And in the spirit of love, we should learn to accept people for who they really are, not who we want them to be.

"And God said, let us make man in our image, after our likeness.." (See Genesis 1:26). "And the Lord God formed man of the dust of the ground, and breathed into his nostrils the breath of life; and man became a living soul." (Genesis 2:7). God took time and special care to make man, therefore God's thoughts of man are special. To get an idea of what this means, consider the love you have for your children and family. We all would like for our children to respect us, and follow our house rules. Some children do follow the rules, and some children don't. (Let's face it, life would be easier if we had more children than do follow the rules than those that don't.) When our children follow the rules, we are happy, and when they disobey, we are sad. And so it is with mankind following God's rules (commandments), God is happy when we are obedient and not pleased when we disobey. Christians should therefore always strive to achieve God's approval by following his commandments.

Most of us have a testimony of thanking God for the

use and activities of our limbs, thanking God for eyes to see, and ears to hear and so on. And some of us say it is hard to live in the Whole Will of God, because we are born into sin. "Wherefore, as by one man sin entered into the world, and death by sin; and so death passed upon all men, for that all have sinned."(Romans 5:12)

As mentioned previously, we should spend quality time with God not only as a family unit, but we should have quality time with God as individuals as well. Spending quality time with God as an individual, will allow you to know and understand what God has planned for you as a person. God wants you to come to Him for everything. That's why it is important that you put God first in your daily life. When we go to work, most of us thank God that we have a job. However, on the other side of the wall, when we are at work, we don't allow God to shine in our lives around our co-workers. We put God on a shelf until we get off work. God should always be first and foremost in our lives as Christians. God's love envelopes mankind such that we might have a right to the tree of life. "He that hath an ear, let him hear what the Spirit saith unto the churches;...."(See Revelation 2:7) We know that when we are working we have to focus on our job, when we're at home we have to focus on things around the house, when in school we have to focus on our lessons, that is given to us because that's a part of this life that we cannot escape. Focusing on God is also a given part of life that we should not neglect. We as believers cannot put God on a shelf while we are going about our everyday activities. The way to keep God on your mind throughout the day is by singing and praying and talking to Him within ourselves.

Let's be honest with ourselves and consider that just because we are born into sin doesn't mean we have to continue in sin. We strife to live the life of what we think is a Christian. However, we make excuses to explain why we can't do right when it's time to step out on the word and the will of God. Instead of adhering to God's word, we make excuses because we lack the love God has in our hearts. God wants us to love Him first, then love one another in spirit and in truth. "Seeing ye have purified your souls in obeying the truth through the Spirit unto unfeigned love of the brethren, see that ye love one another with a pure heart fervently." (1 Peter 1:22) If we love one another the way God wants us to love one another, (and that includes every one God puts on our paths), we will find the capacity to love increasing without bounds. In other words, loving MORE, increases our ability to love MORE.

Every day is a new beginning, so whatever you did yesterday, learn to put it behind you and start each day anew. Everyday is a brand new day that allows us to erase the chalkboard of the past, and start all over. We can not dwell on what happened in the past if we "call" ourselves Christians. While professing to be a Christian, we must remember in daily prayer that His Word, His Will, and His Way (God's) will be done in our lives. God should be the first thing on your mind when you wake up, in your thoughts throughout the day, and the last thing on your mind when you go to sleep. Keeping God in your thoughts can be accomplished by prayer, reciting Psalms, thinking on the things that are of God, singing or otherwise doing something pertaining to God's will, way, or word. We as Christians, cannot get tired of doing the will of God, praising God for what he has done, or showing others the goodness of God's working in our lives. In other words we must let our "light shine before men." (See Matthew 5:15-16) The Bible tells us to think on others as better than ourselves, lest we become ensnared in webs of "pride and conceit." (Philippians 2:3:). We should be nice to everybody and treat everybody the same through the Spirit by the love of God. When someone is spiteful towards you, we must, in the role of loving Christians, treat them with love and kindness, in the hope that our actions will draw them to Christ. Christian's do not render evil for evil but do that which is righteous in the eyes of God. (See 1 Peter 3:9). God will certainly not allow the ones that are fighting against you to overtake you. In such adverse situations, we have to pray to God to give us strength and guidance. A lot of the time when we pray, we ask the Lord to take us away from a situation, rather than asking Him to fix us, so that we will be able to stand fast against whatever the situation or challenge may be. God has the power, and He will be with you until the end no matter what the circumstances. Either way, we know God is by our side, so we should hold on, hold out, go through and be strong.

Love is a sure Foundation,
Love is a solid foundation,
Love is in every nation,
Although it could be individual,
One thing for sure it is spiritual,
Regardless of what time say,
WE need love lest we stray…..
—*Durand Huggins*

As mentioned earlier, almost everybody claims to love their children, but do they really "love" their children? In this respect, when it comes to true love, do we really know and understand what true love means? There was a time in my life when I wondered how one could know if someone truly loved someone else. As the years passed by, and I gained more wisdom and knowledge, I came to realize what love means to me, as well as where love comes from. The Bible tells us that God is love. (See 1 John 4:8) If God is love, how can we truly love without God being a part of our lives?

God wants us to love one another, however, life isn't that easy for some of us. As I mentioned earlier there are many different types of love in the world today. Right now I'm talking about agape love, true love, the love that never fails or ends. To be loved, is what most of us would like from another person, and to be able to return that love is what we hope for when we give love. Now the God of our creation GIVES LOVE whether it is returned or not, in return all He wants from mankind is for us to GIVE OUR LIVES back to Him. He sent His ONLY SON to GIVE HIS LIFE for the sins of mankind. God gave his son as an ultimate expression of love so that man/woman might have life as God intended in the beginning of his creation. He is waiting for us to step into the light of His world, by returning His love. Ever since I can remember, I have heard people say "love is a two-way street". In other words, love is a reciprocal arrangement wherein "you show love to me and I'll show love to you." Someone has to be the first to show love, regardless of how the other person or people feel. When we sing the song of "Oh, how I love Jesus, because he first loved me," we sing it with the belief that Jesus first loved us. We can therefore infer that because Jesus loves us, everybody is born with a little love. If we use that little love that exists in all of us, by giving it to Jesus, He will kindle it and spread it among mankind.

🐚 Conclusion

After reading this book I hope we understand that love comes to God by the Holy Spirit. The only way one can have the Holy Spirit is by repentance of our sins. Then and only then can one gain knowledge of the Fruit of the Holy Spirit. Once one has the Fruit of the Holy Spirit, all nine of the Fruits of the Holy Spirit begin to work in our lives. When one professes to be a Christian, love, joy, peace, long-suffering, goodness, faith, gentleness, meekness, and temperance should all become a part of one's innermost being. One can not serve God with a whole heart without the Fruit of the Holy Spirit working in them. The Fruit of the Holy Spirit also includes showing love not only to ourselves, but to others as well.

Love, above all, is first, because we have to love one another in order to please God. Loving in the manner that God commands us brings on the joy of the Lord which brings joy and strength in your soul. If we keep our minds on Jesus He will keep us in perfect peace. We know there are some things we will go through that are unpleasant, but they can't compare to what Jesus went through as he endured his long-suffering on the cross. We will all have periods of long-suffering in our lives, but after the long-suffering is finished, we can feel good about holding on to the faith that was learned in the process. Long-suffering allows us to understand what it means to be gentle, kind, and meek towards each other.

Temperance is something we all need to work on daily, not only for our sake but for others as well.

When we receive the Holy Spirit within our innermost being, we will know that the Fruit of the Holy Spirit is working within us. During the chaos and disorder of life's most turbulent storms, when there is trouble on every side, one must go to Jesus to seek refuge. During moments of depression, when one may feel a sense of failure, or anxiety, one should open up their heart and tell Jesus all about how they feel. Putting our trust in, and allowing Jesus to come to our rescue, is how we build our faith in Him.

Some people say we can get peace by emptying our minds and meditating every morning until we feel calm. A regimen of daily meditation is also reputed to lower one's stress levels throughout the day. However, realize that peace is not just something in our minds, peace is a way of living. We should "follow peace with all men, and holiness, without which no man shall see the Lord." (Hebrews 12:14). Meditation is good for the soul if it is in the Lord. Reading Isaiah 26: 3, lets us know that God said he would keep us in perfect peace if our minds stayed on Him.

Being good to one another should be natural once one becomes a Christian. Do good things to all even if they don't return your good will. Good overtakes the evil things of life. Good helps keep us to be meek and humble towards one another. Good also brings gentleness in one's life. Life with Christ is joy everlasting. We can be joyful every day of our lives if we just follow Jesus. Going through hard times is a part of everyday life. Living righteous is a change of lifestyle once we become Christians. When we follow a Christian lifestyle, we cease doing the little evil and nasty things we once did. By now we should realize that we cannot and should not try to plow through life alone. We need Christ in our everyday life. That's why Jesus walked the earth to show us how to live Holy for God. Temperance is a way of life as well. We have to learn that although it's okay to be angry, it is not okay to sin while in a state of anger. Always remember that

GOD IS LOVE

BY D. Marie (Writer Name)
denise huggins

Printed in the United States
by Baker & Taylor Publisher Services